THE PARTY ACROSS THE STREET

A SHORT STORY

INCLUDED IN 'YOUR MOTHER'S NIGHTMARES', A
COLLECTION OF SIX TROUBLING TALES

ANITHA KRISHNAN

DREAM PEDLAR BOOKS

For Dhruv,
the greatest miracle in my life.
You came and made my life an adventure. A grand exploration. Of the world outside. And also the world within me. Thank you for this precious gift.

~

For Daiane,
Thank you for showing me that in reality, the house across the street and its residents are absolutely charming and lovely, and nothing at all like my imagination portrayed it in this tale. It's such a blessing to have you here.

~

ABOUT THIS BOOK

The Party Across The Street

When the house across the street swallows up a visitor dressed for a party at 1 a.m., three-year-old Dorian is curious to know more.

Excited at the prospect of an entertaining departure from the monotony of parenting, his sleep-deprived mother accompanies him out the door and across the street to the house where a party is indeed in full swing.

Guests with painted faces and elaborate costumes heartily welcome the mother-son duo, luring them in with the promise of free babysitting and loads of tasty treats.

But no one mentions the presence of a magician in their midst, a magician who knows how to make little children disappear.

BEFORE WE BEGIN

Dear Reader,

Motherhood, or even parenting in general, is one of those life experiences that are almost universal yet remarkably unique to each one of us.

Everyone's parenting journey is vastly different. What works for one parent/family may simply not work for another.

My own journey has been a mix of unimaginable joys and unbelievable anxieties and everything else in between these two extremes.

During those dark moments, I turned to writing as a salve. I couldn't bring myself to speak aloud the fears I had for my child. Already wracked with anxiety and a deep sense of wrongness for even having those fears in the first place, I was terrified that putting them in written or spoken form—by journalling or talking about them to someone—might just make them come true.

Instead, I couched them in the guise of speculative fiction to render them more palatable, more surmountable, and as a reminder that in those moments my fears were exactly that—fiction!

It's for this very reason that I crafted the short story collection, *Your Mother's Nightmares*, a few months ago. *The Party Across The Street* is a short story from that six-tale collection.

If you're a parent, my hope is that in these pages, you too will find the words for the darkness you already know so intimately and grapple with every single day, and emerge into the light on the other side, feeling seen and sane and safe in the knowledge that you are doing the best you can and that is more than enough.

~ *Anitha Krishnan*
Burlington, Ontario,
Monday, 17 June 2024

THE PARTY ACROSS THE STREET

$\mathcal{W}$e are sitting by the living room window overlooking our front lawn, reading *Room On The Broom* by Julia Donaldson and Axel Scheffler, when we see the first guest arrive for the party across the street.

Of course, we don't know for certain there is a party. No invitation was extended to us.

But why else would anyone turn up at another's door at one in the morning wearing a hat with a single tall feather sticking out and a purple cape that looks as if it would make the perfect tent for little Dorian because it is ginormous and lined liberally with tassels and pompoms and has little pinpricks of light, and whether they are night stars or glow worms or spangles, it is difficult to tell?

Although the one big reason it will not make a suitable tent is that it is swallowing the very ground it is trailing on, leaving behind a blackness that looks like it can be anything or nothing at all.

I sneak a quick glance at Dorian. He too is watching. With

the intense curiosity that only three-year-olds can muster. Also with non-judgemental awareness.

His face is impossible to read. There is no fear there. He doesn't yet know of all the impossibilities of life and the laws of physics.

It is as if when I popped him out, he left behind in my womb his entire quota of fear for several lifetimes, and I have been lugging around all the anxiety for both of us ever since, all while trying to not let it contort my face into anything other than intense curiosity (to mask the single-minded alertness) or non-judgemental awareness (to hide the paralyzing panic).

The child watches me more closely than any God has ever done so far.

The first guest climbs up the steps leading to the front door of the house across the street. Bright crimson in daylight, the door is now a rectangular hole darker than the surrounding night.

We don't know who lives in that house. We don't even know that anyone lives there. I have never seen any signs of life in that house. No unexpected twitching of curtains. No windows left open on warm, sunny days. No glow of lights from within when darkness falls.

But, it now strikes me, although I cannot see it presently, its front lawn is always neatly striped. No signs of neglect there. Perhaps the handiwork of an invisible landscape contractor. Or of gnomes.

The door opens to reveal a dim glow of light surrounding the silhouette of the first guest. He steps in, and the door shuts behind him. A sudden bright flash of light erupts from within the house, like a firework set off in silence, and momentarily paints all the windows Halloween-yellow.

Like in a cartoon, three things happen all at once. The roof lifts a little, the windows and the door pop out, and the walls billow like curtains in the wind.

And then a fourth thing. An orange-grey plume of smoke unfurls out of the chimney like a dragon's breath.

I blink, and the house goes dark and still once more. From what I can make out, all the parts of the house have sprung back into place.

"Who was that, Mumma?" Dorian asks.

I let out a breath I only just realize I've been holding. "Hmmm ... I am not sure, sweetie. Who do you think it is?" A question for a question. Stalling tactic. I need time to make sense of it all so I can find the right words to explain without terrifying Dorian. He is not afraid. At least, not in any way that *I* can see. Plus this could be a useful exercise in imagination for him.

"Fiffer-Feffer-Feff," he offers.

My mind's eye conjures up the harmless image of the four-fluffy-feathered funny creature from the book, *Dr. Seuss's ABC*, and, as I toss my head back, an unexpected laughter leaps out of my throat and gambols away on the ether taking some of my disquiet with it.

"Yes, that hat." I acknowledge Dorian's brilliance without resort to excessive, or any, praise.

"Let's go see," Dorian says.

"See what?"

"Not what. Whom," he corrects me. "Fiffer-Feffer-Feff."

"But," I say, and nothing more. Because ... but what? What am I going to say? That it was not really a Fiffer-Feffer-Feff that just sauntered into the invisibly dark house across the street? That I was only being patronizing when I applauded Dorian's observation? That we don't go about wandering the streets at one in the morning? Kill the spirit of curiosity before it has even begun to bloom? Finally, I have it. A way out. "We don't know who lives there, sweetie," I say.

"Why?" he asks.

Why? How does one even begin to answer such a question? Truthfully, I think.

"Well, we have not tried to find out, so we don't know," I answer.

Dorian thinks for a moment. An image of serene thoughtfulness.

"We can go find out now?" he offers. "OK? OK. OK."

That's Dorian. He will ask a question and also give it a favourable answer. *OK? OK. OK.*

He runs to the closet in the entrance hallway and drags out his jacket and boots and mine too. There is no talking him out of this one. Besides, what are my options here? Read *Room On The Broom* twenty or so times before he finally falls asleep? Or head out to what might be a festive occasion, a cause for celebration, filled with adult conversations and, for once, indulge in drinks and food prepared by someone other than me?

"OK. OK." I jump up with enthusiasm, but am unable to muster enough to match his.

2

I help Dorian wear his spring jacket and rain boots, and then run upstairs to change out of yesterday's clothes, stained with spices and finger-paint and coffee.

I opt for a summer dress, a pale yellow affair with a pattern of white lilacs stitched all around the hem. It is funny but I don't remember owning this dress, let alone having ever worn it. It fits me just fine. Whatever.

I sneak a quick glance at the mirror to make sure my hair doesn't look entirely like a bird's nest and my face doesn't look like it simply cannot belong to a human body.

Mission failed. Mirrors suck. They show you the truth without presenting any context, any justification, for it.

Mirror, mirror on the wall,

if you're gonna tell me that my looks appall,

then you better know better than to lie,

when I ask you, do you goddamn know why?

Jeez! Even my three-year old knows 'why', not 'what', is the most important question of all. Sure, he'll first lure me in by asking 'what', but it is the subsequent 'why' that gets him to the truth all the time. And so, remember this: what you see in the mirror is a fraction of the truth, the least important fraction.

"Mummum!" Dorian's voice cuts through my thoughts.

"Coming, sweetie."

I strap on my watch. It is half past one. If a fairy Godmother were to appear in front of me now, never mind the time, I'd ask her to endow a lifetime of restful sleep on me and Dorian, because I really want to sleep. I need to. And so does he.

That is what we both should be doing instead of getting dressed up to knock on the door of a neighbour we have seen not even once since we moved to this suburban neighbourhood more than a year ago.

This entire business, so out of routine, is something I don't want to get involved in, but then I think of the example I'd be setting for Dorian if I were to walk away from this now. My darling Dorian, all dressed up, waiting so patiently for me by the door.

"Mummum?"

"Coming, my precious."

I grab a shawl to wrap around my shoulders, a purchase from another lifetime, a red and maroon and orange affair, the colours of autumn blending in one length of velvety fabric with tiny silvery threads that shimmer with motion. Feet in boots, shawl around shoulders, Dorian's hand in mine, we slip out into the night.

*a*gain, three things happen all at once.

Now the door is in front of us, and then it is gone.

Now the silence of the night is all around us, and then there is music, the rhythmic beats blasting out of the house into the very earth we stand upon, thudding into our hearts.

Now there is no one, and then a bunch of faces appear in front of us, all gorgeously painted in colours I thought only Dorian could concoct by pouring out all his paints on the floor and slip-sliding on them in that singular way that is solely his.

The designs are exquisite. Thought-provoking and comment-worthy. Blue-green whorls and swirls of peacock feathers, black and white spirals you cannot stare at without your head spinning a little, a burgundy sun with green quivering rays like a patient Venus Flytrap.

"Red triangles." Dorian points out, and I see another face painted in concentric triangles, starting from the nose in the centre, in countless shades of red.

A bright red gives way to scarlet and persimmon, flame red merges with vermillion and coral-red, which bleeds into carmine and crimson and cardinal, which merges with rust and burgundy and rosewood and maroon. Like a red triangular sun. Aflame at the centre, giving in to its own darkness pressing all around.

"Good job!" Triangle-Face grins at Dorian, squatting down to peer closer at him, her smile somehow seeming to form yet another triangle. Inverted, though.

"Look, the triangles are moving!" Dorian points a small finger at her, his eyes and mouth like three rings of surprise, as if he too is forming a triangle in response.

"What a clever boy you are!" Triangle-Face is delighted at having found such a keen admirer of her design. "The Devil is always in the details. But don't stare too hard or he'll pop right out and gobble you down!"

Dorian titters. Nervously, I think.

"I'm just kidding!" Triangle-Face pats his cheek. "You clearly know your shapes and colours though. Surely you deserve a treat for getting that right. Would you like some cake?"

Triangle-Face is definitely not a parent or at least not a well-informed one. We are not big on rewards and praises at home. It is all about helping develop a child's inner drive and motivation. Read your Alfie Kohn, babe, I want to admonish her.

And then, as I will find out later, I make my first mistake of the night.

I look at Dorian. His face is lit up. So I keep my mouth shut. Which is why he happily steps towards Triangle-Face and away from me.

Triangle-Face is ecstatic. She scoops him into her arms and sets him on her hips. "Say bye to Mumma," she says, her voice irritatingly high-pitched and childish, and I want Dorian to squirm and whine away from her and back to me. Stranger danger, child? Have I not taught you anything?

"Bye, Mumma," he shouts loud and clear over the sound of the music. "We're going to get some cake."

"What a delightful child he is!" Triangle-Face grins at me. "Is he allergic to anything?"

I am surprised she knows to ask. I mutely shake my head. And off they go.

"*H*e'll be fine," a voice drifts into my ear as a hand gently holds my elbow and Venus Flytrap nudges me into this house in which the light is loud, bright and dark colours drift in and out of a smoky haze, and the music shakes the air within.

The tune is familiar, something I've heard on the car radio too many times to forget, paying too little heed to remember.

"What song is this?" I ask, as we press through a crowd of standing, swaying, moving bodies like branches of a tree casually probing the boughs of its neighbours.

I am not interested in the answer. Not really. I just need to shrug off this emptiness that has replaced Dorian by my side, even in the midst of this crowd, and pretend I am not too worried about him. I don't want to reveal all of this to Venus Flytrap.

The trouble is you never know what might prompt someone to call Social Services on you. You worry too much, you are a clingy parent. You worry too little, you don't care enough to be a good parent. Being a parent is like fighting a losing battle. The only trouble is you can quit fighting only once; that is only when you die.

Anyway, I see Dorian seated beside Triangle-Face at a long table filled with delectable sweetmeats, savouries, and a colourful assortment of cut fruits. That is where we head.

"Starboy," Venus Flytrap says, as she pulls out a chair for me right next to Dorian. He has already heaped his plate with slices of watermelon, mangoes, and oranges beside a thick slice of Black Forest gâteau. He knows the importance of colours in every meal. He now digs into his cake with intent.

I turn to Venus Flytrap absentmindedly. "What?" I ask her, the sight of my child safe and happy, and my proximity to him, stripping me of all the concerns I had nary a moment ago.

"Pardon?" Dorian butts in.

Venus Flytrap smiles and tousles his hair. "The song," she turns to me and says. "You were asking about the song. It is Starboy by The Weeknd."

"The Weekend?"

"Yes," she replies, "but no 'e' before 'n'."

"I want to be Starboy," Dorian declares.

"Sure." I shrug.

"What does starboy mean?" he asks. The 'what' question comes first. I am clueless but I make an attempt.

"I suppose it means a boy who shines like a star." I put my arms up and wiggle them and bring them down in a slow, wide arc, like a cheerleader without the pompoms.

"Why does the boy shine like a star?" That follow-up 'why' question. Entirely expected.

"Maybe if we listened to the song, we might find out everything about the starboy," I suggest.

And that is the second mistake I make that night in that spangled room where disco lights prick the air to the rhythm of the music, and grown-ups with painted faces dance on the floor beside the long table where Dorian and I are feasting.

5

"*A* starboy is someone who is super cool," says a man sliding into the empty chair to my right.

"Fiffer-Feffer-Feff," Dorian shouts.

But the man hardly looks like that beloved creature. The feather on his head is taller than Dorian is. The man (creature?) wiggles his eyebrows, which seems to make his feather sway and dance, much to Dorian's delight.

I look over my shoulder and there it is, that sparkling, earth-swallowing cloak, a piece of night sky for a tail.

"You have a wild imagination, young man," he grins. "But I am actually The Piper." He pulls a flute from somewhere within his cloak and offers it to Dorian. The child promptly puts it into his mouth and blows it like a whistle. The sound is mellifluous but not loud enough to pierce The Weeknd's Starboy still blasting from invisible speakers.

I turn to The Piper. It is only when I look at him closely that I realize I had been expecting the face of a cartoon. A bulbous nose and a wide mouth set in a face that should have stretched like elastic. Or something like that.

But no. Here is a man whose face is a study in geometry. All sharp angles and smooth planes, sparkling like a polished gemstone in the glimmer of the disco lights, as if he has swallowed the sun and the light is now shimmering through the pores of his skin. Clearly, I have been reading too many vampire stories on my Kindle during sleepless nights.

"Starboy is a great nickname for Dorian then," I say, using conversation to distract myself from staring at The Piper.

"Yes," he affirms, "although it is also a synonym for Casanova."

I promptly wonder if I should discourage Dorian from nicknaming himself Starboy. But I have also learnt that as far as Dorian is concerned, the forbidden fruit must be tasted, and the forbidden act must be carried out.

"Would you like to see a magic trick?" The Piper asks Dorian.

The child spoons some cake into his mouth and nods.

The Piper springs up from his chair and comes around me, then grabs one end of his glittering cloak and throws it over Dorian. I jump up but The Piper lays a heavy hand on my shoulder and keeps me glued to my seat, as he pulls back his cloak to reveal an empty space where Dorian was a moment ago.

"What the f—?" I begin but The Piper lays a finger on his lips and winks at me. If his gesture is meant to assuage me, it has the opposite effect.

I reach out to grab his cloak but he is swifter than I am. He swishes his cloak over the chair once again and drags it back to reveal Dorian back in his place on the chair, staring up at something.

"Whoa!" The child blinks at us. I grab Dorian and hug him, both relieved and embarrassed, as he squirms out of my grip to face The Piper.

"How do you feel?" I ask Dorian, as casually as I can in the face of what has just transpired. He has the nose of a hound when it comes to smelling desperation and fear. I give him a quick visual once-over. He appears unharmed, both physically and emotionally.

"Happy," he says.

"What did you see?" I ask, injecting some excitement into the question.

"Moon," Dorian says, his eyes glancing at the ceiling as if to coax whatever he had seen under the cloak back into existence. "Stars. Millions of stars. Billions of stars." He then turns to The Piper and asks, "How did you do that?"

"It's a secret." The Piper puts a finger to his lips. "Never tell anyone I keep a piece of night sky hidden in my cloak."

Dorian nods at The Piper in solemn understanding. "Yes," he says, and turns towards his plate. Unfinished business to attend to.

My breath is short and rapid, and my heart is still thudding for a way out of my chest, but it all appears to have been a harmless trick, at least as far as Dorian is concerned. Every moment of anxiety pertaining to him leaves me a little more permanently damaged than before.

The Piper bends over to me and smiles. "My apologies," he says. "I should have warned you."

"Yes, you should have." I am miffed. I also hate it when people apologize for their mistakes before I've had the opportunity to let my anger at their behaviour run its course.

"My apologies again." He bows and extends his hand. "Please allow me to make it up to you with a dance," he offers.

The absurd timing of his proposal makes me groan inwardly. No way do I want to dance with a man who just made my three-year-old child disappear from right under my nose. In fact, I should be running out of this party place and back to our home right now. That is the sensible thing to do, isn't it?

I glance at Dorian, as if a shoulder angel hovers over him, bearing the answers to all the important questions of this Universe. He is attempting to squish a pulp of mango into The Piper's flute. I do not bother to dissuade him. The Piper deserves this for the torment he has caused me. But would it not be in poor taste to thwart his attempt at an apology, no matter how ludicrous?

Triangle-Face and Venus Flytrap are locked in deep conversation on the other side of Dorian but they throw occasional glances at him. Assured they are keeping an eye on my child, I take off my shawl and drape it gently around his shoulders. Something of mine for him to hold on to in my absence.

And then I make the third mistake of the evening as I slip my hand into The Piper's and let him lead me away from the table, away from Dorian, into a slow dance, one hand held snugly in his, another on his shoulder, his arm draped around my waist and resting on the small of my back, firm yet gentle, Starboy having given way to a slow, lilting melody in which the music is not interrupted by lyrics. My skin starts to tingle as if some of The Piper's luminescence is permeating me.

"So, are you a starboy?" I ask him. I am still mad at him for making Dorian vanish.

He throws his head back and laughs. "It doesn't matter, does it?"

"You being a starboy?"

"Whether I am one or not?"

I smile and shake my head. I turn to look at Dorian, who is playing a game with Venus Flytrap. He points at her nose with his index finger just an inch away from her face, and promptly pulls it back as she springs her trap shut. He is quick, that child, and also a good sport.

"He seems to be a great kid," The Piper says.

"Oh, he's an absolute delight," I declare, still watching Dorian laugh as I sway in The Piper's arms.

"It must be hard, caring for a child," he says, with an unexpected softness on his face.

This is where conversations on parenting get tricky. To admit something is hard is almost akin to wishing you didn't have to do it. And yes, there are days I wish I weren't a mother.

But to admit it is hard without acknowledging it is beautiful too is like speaking a half-truth. Like a mirror presenting a fact without context.

And yet, to deny it is arduous is unthinkable. It is the kind of lie that can pull the rug from under unsuspecting feet, break hopeful hearts, banish faith, and instil fear in the minds of countless others like me.

Whether it is the shock of seeing Dorian disappear or the fact that no one has really commiserated with me until now for the difficulties of parenting, I say what I've never said to anyone else.

"It is. It is very hard. And many days I just want to give up. I wish for nap-times to never end. I wish for the morning to never come, just so that I can remain buried under the sheets. And yet, on other days, I think that all the magic of this Universe has manifested itself in the form of this precious child."

"No parent truly deserves their child, you know," The Piper sighs.

I turn back to him. "What do you mean?" I ask, although I can guess. If we believe we should not suffer the way we do for our children, then we also cannot lay claim to the unexpected marvels that come with watching a life bloom. I suppose that is what God must have felt during the creation of this Universe.

"Children come into this world, whole and pure, sacred and divine," The Piper explains. "Unfortunately, they are born to adults who are broken, who have strayed from their true selves. Surely, no adult has the means to preserve the sanctity of a child."

"That may very well be," I empathize. "But everybody was once a child. And who better than a child to remind us of that?"

The Piper narrows his eyes and asks, "Does that make you bitter? Remembering that you too were once as joyful, as uninhibited, but no longer are?"

I scoff. "On the contrary, I am delighted to have found my way back to what really matters, to who really matters."

I am beginning to feel a little annoyed with his judgements. True, the desires of an adult and the needs of a child remain in near constant conflict. But isn't that the crux of parenting? Finding a way to handle the duality of it all? Isn't that the essence of life?

The Piper smirks. "It can't be that simple. Sure, he's a

delight at this age, but you do know what they say about those teenage years, right? That is when most parents fail their children. Spectacularly."

I pull my hands away and step back from The Piper. "Are you a parent?" I ask him.

"I fund an orphanage," he says. "But no, I don't look after the children myself."

"That is a noble thing to do," I say because what I really find noble is his admission that he completely lacks parenting skills and has no basis, whatsoever, to judge the parenting choices that real parents like me have to make every day, every moment. But, of course, he does not get that.

"Yeah, I ended up with a bunch of kids and no grown-ups on my street. I was barely an adult myself back then. So I put them up in this empty house and hired a few hands to cook and clean."

"What happened to their parents?"

"Nothing happened to them," he wiggles his fingers in the air to form quotation marks around his utterance of the word 'happened'. "They were just the type of people who didn't deserve their children," he shrugs, as if helplessly.

A tiny terror forms a lump in my throat. "What do you mean?" I croak.

"They were cheats who didn't keep their word," he shakes his head ruefully. "No child deserves to grow up with such parents."

Something stirs in the back of my mind. A piper and his pipe. Children gone missing. Parents who didn't keep their word. I gasp. "Are you The Pied Piper of Hamelin?" I shout.

"The one and only," he smiles, and for the first time that evening I see how ugly and menacing a smile can be.

His razor-sharp looks are like a thousand blades piercing my skin. An unknown fear grips my body and I push past the dancing bodies and run towards the table faster than my mind can conjure up the thought fully.

But I am too late.

Dorian is gone.

6

*I*n that house across the street from mine, where guests with painted faces feasted and danced to the rhythm of light and music only a moment ago, is now a silence, emptier but heavier than the darkness that has settled everywhere. That house is now like a hole in space and time.

A match is struck.

A candle is lit and placed on the table, now bereft of all the delicacies that had lured Dorian in like a moth to a flame.

Three fake faces glow in the candlelight, monstrous shadows flicker on the walls behind.

"Where is Dorian?" I scream and hurl myself at Triangle-Face, who is nearest to me.

I don't even reach her before the trio jumps up. Hands grab me and pin me to a chair. A rope is produced and used to bind me securely, even as I flail and kick around. The struggle is futile. The three settle back into their seats and watch me squirm.

"What have you done with him?" I yell. Hot tears run down my cheeks and neck.

"Nothing yet," The Piper says, twiddling with his pipe. "It all depends on you."

"What do you mean?" I snarl.

"You made three mistakes this evening," he says. "And that has cost you dearly."

"What mistakes?" I look around at all three of them but Venus Flytrap and Triangle-Face sit with no voice in their throats and no emotion on their painted faces.

"First," The Piper explains, sticking out the index finger on his right hand, "you permitted your child to partake of food offered by a stranger. Second," he sticks out his middle finger, "you allowed him to listen to songs completely inappropriate for anyone his age. And third, you simply left him with strangers just so you could seduce another stranger."

I nearly gag at his final accusation. He waggles his counting fingers at me with the kind of ill-placed delight a despotic principal would find in caning the palms of errant students.

I rack my brains for some acerbic retort, some witty comeback, but am choked with the absurdity of it all.

Sure, accuse me of bringing a sleepless Dorian to a never-before-seen neighbour's home at one in the morning only to stumble into a party filled with food and people and music.

But if accepting a man's request to dance because *he* wants to apologize is tantamount to me seducing him, then one of us is entirely in the wrong Universe at the wrong time in history.

I look at the trio, The Piper pacing up and down, Venus Flytrap and Triangle-Face sitting still as stones, all watching me, waiting for the next words to spill out of my mouth, mentally spinning the next web of lies and deceit to trap me in.

They are the only ones in this room now, the only ones who know where Dorian is, and that is all that matters, I tell myself. Not their judgements, not their insinuations.

I want to scream and shout and rant about how crazy they are and how unfair their accusations are.

But if there is one thing I've learnt in the past three years of looking after Dorian and fending off well-intentioned advice from unexpected quarters, it is this: it is almost impossible to argue someone out of their staunch beliefs.

And so I say, employing the calm and empathetic tone I have learnt to use because of Dorian, my darling Dorian, "I am sorry. I trusted you all even though, as you say," I nod towards The Piper, "you are only strangers to me. I trusted you the way I trust that Starbucks will not poison the banana bread I order for Dorian. I left him with you two," I look at Triangle-Face and Venus Flytrap, "and stepped not more than six feet away because he seemed comfortable with you. As for the song, I don't even know the lyrics to judge whether it is age-appropriate or not."

The Piper snorts, then slams a palm on the table. His theatrics have the desired effect of terrifying me.

"*Ignorantia neminem excusat,*" he says, pointing a finger at me. I don't need to ask him what it means. Ignorance is no excuse.

My undergrad professor of Corporate Ethics used to repeat a similar phrase so often it is quite literally the only thing I remember from the course I took in what must have been another lifetime.

Ignorantia legis neminem excusat. Ignorance of the law is no excuse.

The ridiculousness of it all makes me want to laugh. These three hypocrites here, not one with the balls to bring up a child. And I, bound to this chair, as if I were on trial for the neglect and abuse of my own.

"Where is my child?" I muster the courage to ask. "Clearly you are as concerned for him as I am. He must be terrified, wherever he is."

The Piper narrows his eyes. *"Ignorantia sit beatitudo,"* he says. Ignorance is bliss.

But who is ignorant, I wonder? Is he saying I am better off not knowing where Dorian is? Or that Dorian, wherever he may be, is completely oblivious to the goings-on here?

More tears spill from my eyes and I am unable to put up a façade of calmness anymore.

"I'll do anything to get him back, please," I whimper. "We all make mistakes. I'll be more careful henceforth. I promise."

The Piper looks at Venus Flytrap and Triangle-Face, who nod back at him. "You must answer a question then," he declares.

"Of course," I reply, sensing a glimmer of hope. Truth or dare? Seriously? Anyway, there is nothing so abominable in my past that I can't reveal it to bring back Dorian. "Ask me anything, please," I say, blinking back tears.

"You will have only one opportunity to answer." The Piper waggles his index finger again at me. "So think carefully before you speak."

"Sure." I nod fervently. Game on.

"Which of the three of us has Dorian?" The Piper asks.

My heart stops for one long instant.

"Which ... one ... of ... the ... three ... of ... us ... has ... Dorian?" The Piper repeats his question, spacing out the words for emphasis, and smirks.

The several implications of this question dawn upon me all at once.

The Piper has just admitted that one of the three of them has Dorian. There is no indication yet as to the state Dorian is in but considering how fanatic this self-righteous trio is when it comes to childcare, I assume that, at the very least, Dorian is physically unharmed.

Of course, he will not escape the trauma of this episode for the rest of his life but he'll have me by his side through all the nightmares and panic attacks that lie in wait for us. But right now, relief floods through me and I feel light enough to fly, were it not for the rope binding me to the chair.

And then the improbability of answering this question hits me like deadweight on my head.

Think, I command my brain.

Whodunnit?

Think!

I frantically bring up my memories of this bizarre evening thus far and search for clues. It is all a jumble. The painted faces, the strobing lights, the pulsing music, the dancers and the feast. Now that everything else has disappeared, it is hard to believe they were even here in the first place.

I look around. There is nothing but darkness punctuated by the flickering shadows of this ghastly trio dancing on the wall behind, even as two of them sit motionless like mountains and one continues to pace up and down, twirling his flute in his hand, as if immobility were anathema to him.

The flute! Hadn't he passed it on to Dorian before the dance?

I peer at it. There is nothing much to see. It appears clean. No mango pulp sticking out from one end.

When and how did The Piper retrieve it? He was dancing with me the entire time. Unless, maybe it wasn't him?

It could just as easily have been either of the other two, or the two of them in unison. But what were The Piper's words, the second time he posed his question?

Which one of the three of us has Dorian? I clearly remember he waggled a finger at me when he said 'one' for emphasis.

Or am I simply making a collage of memories in my head and force-fitting snippets of recollections into a path to lead me to a logical answer, when this whole situation is entirely bereft of sense and sanity?

I look at Venus Flytrap and remember the game of trap Dorian was playing with her. That was the last time I saw him. The realization makes me sick. I just want to get him back and get the hell out of here with him.

I might as well be taking a test and attempting to pen a thousand-word essay with only two minutes to spare, entirely aware of the futility of it all yet desperate to notch up my word count as much as possible.

But I also remember how good Dorian was at evading the trap.

No. It could not have been Venus Flytrap.

I remember from a *National Geographic Kids* magazine Dorian and I were browsing through in the library the other day that this carnivorous plant only traps insects and arachnids. Obviously, Dorian is neither.

I turn to Triangle-Face and stare into her eyes, seeking a clue, but I'm unable to look at her for longer than a few moments without feeling dizzy. It is as if I am endlessly falling into an optical illusion even though I remain exactly where I was several moments ago. Tied and bound to a chair in the house across the street from mine.

Triangle-Face was the one who had led Dorian straight to the table of goodies. Did she slip something into his Black Forest cake? A drug to make him drowsy, perhaps? Something to knock him out so they could quietly and swiftly slip him away in those few moments when I dared to look away?

These thoughts twirl endlessly in my mind until every new thought that springs up is no longer new, but very old and worn-out because of being repeatedly twisted and turned over in my head.

My throat is parched. My breath is swift and shallow. I feel an intense need for physical movement to stop this churning in my head.

I am staring too hard into the lines of thoughts zinging through my brain like a school of fish darting incessantly in all directions.

Don't stare too hard. Step back and reassess, I tell myself.

That's when it hits me.

Don't stare too hard.

Isn't that what Triangle-Face had remarked to Dorian at the door when he had observed her moving triangles?

The Devil is in the details. He'll pop right out and gobble you down!

Triangles. Devil.

The Devil's Triangle!

A lesson in geography from a very long time ago. What

was it called? The Bermuda Triangle. That's it. Where everything disappears, without any explanation.

But what if I am wrong?

I am terrified. I look at the three of them once more.

The Piper.

Venus Flytrap.

Triangle-Face.

If I had to choose one of them to look after Dorian, whom would I trust the most?

The Piper shows no remorse for luring children away from their parents.

Venus Flytrap was more inclined to talk about the music than about the anxiety that was pounding through my chest as Dorian was being led away from me within moments of our stepping into this dastardly house.

Triangle-Face did try to terrify my child with her talk of the Devil but promptly admitted it was a joke. Was that a warning?

Don't stare too hard.

What would Dorian have done? Of course, he would have tried to stare harder than was humanly possible. That was no warning from her. It was an invitation. Harmless on the face of it, but enough to entice any inquisitive child.

"Triangle-Face!" I shout before I can think anymore and invalidate my most recent hypotheses.

Time skids to a halt. The Piper freezes mid-stride. Venus Flytrap pauses mid-breath. Only Triangle-Face exhales, as though letting go of a breath held for far too long.

But before she can utter a word, The Piper hurls his cloak over all of us.

I instinctively close my eyes. A darkness smothers me. I hear a shuffling. And then, a soft cry.

"Mumma!" A shout right into my ears.

Dorian! So close! But I can't see a thing.

I flail my arms and legs to free myself from the ropes, but I'm strangely swathed in what feels like fabric.

I open my eyes. The night sky has fallen on my face. I push it away and try to hold it up. Silver stars shimmer in it, tinier than pinpricks.

Only, as my eyes adjust to the darkness, I see it is no longer black. Strips of red and maroon and orange merge and un-merge above me. What first looked like stars are no longer star-shaped. They look like tiny filaments. Confetti left over from a party.

I claw at this thing, whatever it is—it feels like fabric—and pull it away from me.

An avalanche of light blinds my eyes, and it takes me a few moments to realize it is the sunlight pouring from the east-facing window of Dorian's bedroom.

I whip my head around, and there is his three-year-old face, peering into mine with inquisitive eyes. My heart is pounding, but I try to stay calm and not alarm him.

"Wake up, Mumma," he says. "It's morning."

"Are you alright? How are you feeling?" I ask him, gently dragging him into a hug and hoping he will not discern the insane pace at which my heart is racing and inquire about it.

What I really want to do is squeeze him into a tight embrace, give him a hug so tight that he becomes tiny again, a foetus I can carry forever in my uterus without fear of losing him to unhinged strangers in this mad, mad world.

"Yes, I am OK," he says. "Are you alright?" Always the copycat.

"Of course, I am, sweetie," I say, wondering what he remembers of the previous night and how I can coax it out of him without sending the alarm bells ringing, which would be sure to shut him up.

"Did you sleep well?" I ask, pulling back to scrutinize him surreptitiously. He looks just fine. Bright-eyed and alert, as if he's had a good night's sleep.

He nods, then pouts. "But you didn't finish reading the book."

"Which one?"

Room On The Broom." He jumps up and reaches for the book, which now lies by the side of his floor-bed. "Read it now," he says, thrusting it into my hands. Surely, the child is unharmed?

I need to know what he remembers, and so I ask, "Oh, why did we not finish reading it last night, honey?"

"Because we had a party," he says. "Now read it."

"Did we now?" Dread pools in the pit of my stomach but I only display an acceptable moderate level of interest on my face.

"Yes. Read it, please."

"Where was the party?"

"In the kitchen. Now, read the book, Mumma." I hear the beginning of a whine.

I am almost tempted to threaten him that I will not read the book unless he tells me everything he can remember. Is he traumatized by everything that happened? And where the hell had that crazy trio hidden him when they were torturing me? So I change tack.

"Did we have cake at the party?"

He nods. "Black Forest," he volunteers. "It is my favourite."

"Who gave you cake?"

"You gave me," he says. "Now read it, please."

Dorian inherits his stubbornness from me. I want the answers to all my questions as badly as he wants me to read the book. And his responses seem to suggest he has a recollection of an entirely different party altogether. One that I am sure did not take place. I push as far as I can.

"Did anyone else come to our party?" I ask.

"No, Mumma," he is exasperated now. "It was just you, me, and the cake. Now read the book ple-ee-ee-ease."

I wonder if the three crazy creatures we encountered last evening have somehow altered Dorian's memory so that all he remembers about the incident are only the good bits of it, and not the horrifying parts. I make one last attempt.

"Was Fiffer-Feffer-Feff at the party?" I ask.

Dorian thinks, silently.

"Like in that book, Dr. Seuss's ABC?" I add.

Dorian shakes his head. "I don't know," he says.

There, I have lost him. *I don't know* is sometimes the child's equivalent of *I don't want to talk about it*. I have pushed too far. Or perhaps, he sincerely does not know. Either way, I have no recourse now but to drop the conversation and read *Room On The Broom*.

7

We come down to make breakfast after having read the book four times.

First, I head into the living room and look out of the window to see if the house across the street from ours is still standing or, like Dorian's recollection of last night's adventures, has changed into something else entirely. A swimming pool. A tennis court. Or a restaurant, perhaps?

Nope. No such luck.

It is still there.

The front lawn is still tame, refusing to grow wild. The crimson door remains closed, as if it is not a real door but merely an image of one painted on the wall.

Nothing twitches. Nothing explodes. Nothing seems amiss.

I wonder if I can ever sit by the window and look out without recalling the horrors of the night. Not even half a day has gone by since I lost my child, albeit temporarily, and found him again by some uncanny stroke of luck.

Was it really Triangle-Face who had hidden him? And if so, where?

Does Dorian really not remember anything as it all happened?

Or does he remember only the bits he wants to? The bits that matter to him? Like the joy of a party? Cake?

Or is this some sort of merciful act by the trio? Did they only want to scare the bejesus out of me but ensure my child was not harmed in any way?

Perhaps, the past is nothing but all the stories we tell ourselves. About ourselves. About others. About everything that has transpired.

Maybe I should stop harping on about how I lost Dorian, almost forever, and instead think about how I got him back. Whether it was by a stroke of pure luck or indeed some strategic thinking on my part, I will never know.

Somewhat troubled, somewhat relieved, I turn away from the living room window and head into the kitchen, where Dorian has already climbed on to the countertop, awaiting his breakfast.

I pour some readymade pancake mix into a bowl and add water to form the batter. It occurs to me I ought to serve him something healthier, like eggs and fruits, in the mornings. Tomorrow is another day, I tell myself and sigh.

"Mumma," Dorian's voice chirps up. "Shall we ask Alexa to play songs?"

"Sure!" I am thrilled my child can find ways to keep himself entertained when I am otherwise occupied.

"Alexa," he calls out.

The rim of the cylindrical gadget lights up in a dancing blue that runs along the perimeter a few times.

Satisfied that he has Alexa's full attention, my three-year-old commands, "Alexa, play Starboy by The Weeknd."

~

Ready for more fantasy short stories on the motherhood experience? Check out the collection, Your Mother's Nightmares: Six Troubling Tales, which includes five more twisted tales on the motherhood experience.

When you buy the collection directly from my store, please treat yourself to a 40% discount using the code YMN40.

Please note the code YMN40 is valid only for the short story collection — Your Mother's Nightmares: Six Troubling Tales — in ebook format when purchased directly from my PayHip store, Dream Pedlar Books.
Go to https://payhip.com/b/SfQvj to redeem your code!

ENJOYED THE PARTY ACROSS THE STREET?

Thank you for reading *The Party Across The Street*!

If you loved the story, I hope you will consider writing a short review—even a simple line or two—on the site where you bought the book.

Publishing is still driven by word of mouth, and when you leave a review it helps other readers decide this is a story worth reading. Thank you for your help in spreading the word.

∾

You can also sign up to my monthly newsletter for updates on new book releases as well as heartfelt reflections on writing, reading, parenting and living the creative life.

Monthly Missives from The Dream Pedlar
https://thedreampedlar.com/newsletter

AUTHOR'S NOTE

Dear Reader,

We first moved to Burlington, Ontario, in the spring of 2018. It was my initiation into living the suburban life in North America.

In those initial weeks and months, I was constantly taken aback by the fact that you could live right next-door to someone and yet not see them for days and weeks on end.

The windows in the living room of our townhome overlooks a small front lawn, beyond which is a private road. The other side of the road is flanked by a row of backyards of another set of townhomes.

The house directly opposite mine seemed unoccupied. They only had a short wire fence, which offered me a direct view into their backyard and kitchen window. I never saw any signs of life in there.

But strangely, their backyard was impeccably tidy in the summers. The lawn was mowed. The plants were trimmed. I've never found out how they—whoever 'they' were— managed that.

The only rational explanation I have is that whoever came to tend to their backyard must have done so quickly and quietly when I wasn't looking (which was most of the day, by the way, in case you were wondering).

D (my child, Dhruv) was barely two years old when we moved to this neighbourhood. As a stay-at-home mom, I was constantly lonely and always worrying whether I was doing enough for my child.

I couldn't reconcile the blissful innocence of a child with the surprising ugliness the world seems to be capable of. How could one thrive in the midst of the other?

I remember when I got my driving license a few months later and began to take D to community centres and play areas farther than we could get to on bike. On one of these car journeys, The Weeknd's *Starboy* started to play on the radio.

I loved the song so much that I let it play, assuming D wouldn't understand the explicit nature of the lyrics anyway. That indeed turned out to be the case, but later I felt a pang of terrible guilt at having exposed my baby to explicit language.

My maternal brain and my wild imagination made an explosive combination in those days. I was always worried that someone would scold me for these little 'oversights' instead of giving myself a pat on the back for putting in the effort to be a conscious and peaceful (although not perfect) parent to D.

Anyhoo, the sight of the definitely empty house across the street from ours, my constant feeling of inadequacy as a parent, and the heart-rending lyrics of *Starboy* by The Weeknd fell into a magical kaleidoscope and yielded the short story you now know as *The Party Across The Street*.

(On an aside, I'm a huge fan of The Weeknd. As a

contemporary artist, he is so prolific and his songs are so varied in nature, his body of work inspires me to experiment with my own writings and let each story take me wherever it wants to. He's a great inspiration to me.)

In early 2020, another neighbour said to us that that house was sold, and that the new family that had moved in had a little boy who was the same age as mine and another wee one was on the way. We were excited at the thought of a playmate right across from our home.

Only, the pandemic followed. And shortly after moving in, the family had their wire fence taken down and replaced with a tall wooden fence. Occasionally, I heard the sounds of children playing in the yard, but they disappeared as quickly as they come.

I did meet the family once on a walk around the neighbourhood. And that was it. I didn't think I'd recognize any of them if our paths were to cross at the neighbourhood park or the grocery store.

For almost four years, it just didn't occur to me that I could simply walk around to their front door and introduce myself. Because if I did, I could no longer indulge in moaning about the isolation of living in a North American suburb, could I?

Everything changed after a chance meeting during a walk along the neighbourhood bike path a couple of months ago. As of the time of writing this, the two families have met and delighted in each other's company several times. Now we have many playdates, celebrate birthdays together, and enjoy many moments of happiness!

Funny how the world can turn on its head if only we take a chance.

Thank you for reading this far. I'd love to stay in touch with you. And I hope you'd like to stay connected with me too.

I send out a monthly newsletter on the last Sunday of every month filled with heartfelt musings on the joys of writing, reading and living the creative life. Subscription is free.

You will be the first to hear of my forthcoming works. I also include updates on my writing life, book recommendations, free short fiction, and occasional surprises.

Thank you for staying with me this far. If you choose to accompany me further on this journey, I promise you a magical ride.

Climb aboard at https://thedreampedlar.com/newsletter!

~ Anitha Krishnan
Burlington, Ontario
Monday, 17 June 2024

MORE BOOKS BY ANITHA KRISHNAN

https://thedreampedlar.com/books/

Dying Wishes

Finalist, 2023 Rakuten Kobo Emerging Writer Prize in Speculative Fiction

A contemporary fantasy novel weaving Hindu mythology and South Indian folklore into a quest for belonging across different worlds — the World of Mortals and the World of Gods, India and Canada, the past and the present, the world outside and the one within.

Erased from Existence

A paranormal mystery in which a fifteen-year-old is erased from the memories and perception of everyone. Trapped in oblivion, she will have to unearth and reveal long-buried family secrets to escape.

The Land of No Reflection

A fantasy tale of two sightless young women on the run from their homeland, having committed the unpardonable crime of seeing.

A Benevolent Goddess

A story of a goddess who is punished for her desire to help human beings but is unable to find salvation by any other means.

In Search of Leo

A fantasy tale exploring the gamut of emotions that loss and grief can stir.

The Mind Meddler

A short fantasy story on the games The Mind Meddler plays by sneaking thoughts into people's minds, until he meets the one person who can resist his unkind mischief.

Mrs. D'Souza's Dispute With God

A fantasy short story in which a school teacher, Mrs. D'Souza, dies unexpectedly and sets out in search of God to demand answers to her burning questions on life and death.

Hello, Dreamer! Poems & Dreams

An eclectic collection of 100 short poems encompassing musings on the universe and its mysteries, nature and human life, my secret longings and fears, love and heartbreak, the sun and the moon, the stars and the seas, light and shadow, and joy and nostalgia.

ABOUT THE AUTHOR

Anitha Krishnan is a speculative fiction author and an award-winning poet. Her fantasy novel, *Dying Wishes*, was a finalist for the 2023 Rakuten Kobo Emerging Writer Prize in the Speculative Fiction category.

She has lived in and left pieces of her heart in many places across the world including Singapore, Australia, Canada, and most of all in her beloved birthplace, India. She presently lives in Burlington, Ontario with her husband and their cherished child.

Find more books and her blog on the writing life at
https://thedreampedlar.com.

Sign up to her monthly newsletter at
https://thedreampedlar.com/newsletter
to receive heartfelt musings, exclusive updates, book recommendations, free fiction, and more!